INCIDENTS

INCIDENTS

☾

ROLAND BARTHES

TRANSLATED BY

RICHARD HOWARD

UNIVERSITY OF CALIFORNIA PRESS

BERKELEY   LOS ANGELES   OXFORD

University of California Press
Berkeley and Los Angeles, California
University of California Press, Ltd.
Oxford, England
© 1992 by
The Regents of the University of California
Printed in the United States of America
9 8 7 6 5 4 3 2 1

NOTE FROM THE PUBLISHER

The four texts here translated were originally published in France, seven years after the death of their author, by Éditions du Seuil under the collective title Incidents *(1987). "La lumière du Sud-Ouest" and "Au Palace ce soir . . ." first appeared in* L'Humanité *(1977) and* Vogue-Hommes *(1978), respectively. "Incidents" and "Soirées de Paris" had not previously been published.*

Library of Congress Cataloging-in-Publication Data

Barthes, Roland.
    [Incidents. English]
    Incidents / Roland Barthes ; translated by Richard Howard.
      p.   cm.
    Translation of: Incidents.
    ISBN 0-520-07104-2 (paper : alk. paper)
    1. Barthes, Roland.   2. Linguists—France—Biography.
3. Critics—France—Biography.   I. Title.
P85.B33A3   1992
410'.92—dc20
[B]   91-45211

CONTENTS

♪

THE LIGHT OF THE SUD-OUEST

1

INCIDENTS

11

AT LE PALACE TONIGHT...

43

SOIRÉES DE PARIS

49

THE LIGHT OF
THE SUD-OUEST

T ODAY, JULY 17, the weather is splendid. Sitting on the garden bench and squinting so as to obliterate all perspective, the way children do, I see a daisy in the flowerbed, flattened against the meadow on the other side of the road.

This road flows past like a calm river; occasionally traveled by a motorbike or a tractor (those are the real sounds of the country now, ultimately no less poetic than birdsong: infrequent, they emphasize nature's silence and stamp it with the discreet signs of human activity), the road will irrigate a whole outlying district of the village. For modest though it is, this village has its eccentric districts. Isn't the village, in France, always a contradictory space? Limited, centered, it nonetheless extends quite far; mine, quite classically, has one square, one church, one bakery, one pharmacy, two grocery stores (I should say, today, two supermarkets); but it also has—a sort of caprice that flouts the apparent laws of human geography—two barbers and two doctors. France, the country of the *juste milieu*? Rather—and this on all levels of national life—the country of complex proportions.

My Sud-Ouest is similarly extensible, like the daisy and like all images that change their meaning with the level of perception where I choose to locate them. For example, I can identify, subjectively, three Sud-Ouests.

The first is enormous (a fourth of France), and a stubborn feeling of solidarity instinctively identifies it for me (I have certainly never visited all of it): any news reaching me from this space touches me in a personal way. Upon reflection, it seems that what unifies this great Sud-Ouest is its language: not the dialect (for I know no *langue d'oc*) but the accent, doubtless because the Sud-Ouest accent has formed the models of intonation that marked my earliest childhood. I distinguish this Gascon accent (broadly speaking) from the other meridional accent, that of the Mediterranean Midi, which in today's France has something triumphant about it: a whole folklore of cinema (Raimu, Fernandel), advertising (olive oil, lemon juice), and tourism supports it; the Sud-Ouest accent (heavier perhaps, not so lilting) lacks these tokens of modernity; only interviews with football players serve to illustrate it. I myself have no accent; from childhood, though, I have retained one "meridionalism": I say "socializme" and not "socialissme" (who knows, maybe that makes two socialisms?).

My second Sud-Ouest is not a region, merely a line, a lived trajectory. Whenever I drive down from Paris (I have made this trip a thousand times) I pass Angoulême, where there is a signal that tells me I have crossed the threshold and am entering the country of my childhood; a pine grove on one side of the road, a palm tree in a courtyard, a certain height of the clouds that gives the terrain the mobility of a face. Then begins the great light of the Sud-Ouest, noble and subtle at the same time; never gray, never low (even when the sun is not shining), it is light-as-space, defined less by the colors it imparts to things (as in the other Midi) than by the eminently *habitable* quality it communicates to the earth. I find no other way of saying it: it is a luminous light. You must see this light (I would almost say: hear it, so musical is its quality) in autumn, which is the sovereign season of this country; liquid, radiant, heartrending since it is the last fine light of the year, illuminating each thing in its difference (the Sud-Ouest is the country of microclimates), it saves this country from all vulgarity, from all "gregarity" too, making it inapt for facile tourism and revealing its profound aristocracy (not a question of class but of character). Offering such tribute, I catch myself wondering: are there never disagreeable moments in this Sud-Ouest weather? Of course, but for me these are not the (quite frequent) moments of rain or storm; not even the times when the sky is overcast; the accidents of light, here, seem to engender no spleen; they do not affect the "soul," only the body, sometimes sticky with humidity, intoxicated with chlorophyll, or languid, exhausted by the wind from Spain that brings the Pyrénées so close, so purple: an ambiguous sentiment, in which fatigue ultimately has something delicious about it, as happens each time it is my body (and not my gaze) that is stirred.

My third Sud-Ouest is even smaller: it is the city where I spent my childhood, later my vacations as an adolescent (Bayonne), it is the village to which I return every year, it is the trajectory that unites the two and that I have covered so many times, to buy cigars or stationery in town, or to meet a friend at the station. I have a choice of several roads;

the longer one crosses the fields through a landscape hybridized between Béarn and Basque country; another, a delicious country road, follows the crest of the hills above the Adour; on the other side of the river, I see a continuous bank of trees, dark in the distance: these are the pines of Les Landes; a third, quite recent road (dating from this year) threads its way along the left bank of the Adour: of no interest, except for the speed of the journey and an occasional glimpse of the broad, gentle river studded with the little white sails of a yacht club. But my favorite road, which I often indulge myself by taking, is the one that follows the right bank of the Adour; this is an old towpath, passing many farms and fine houses. I probably like it so much because it is so natural, with that balance of nobility and familiarity so characteristic of the Sud-Ouest; you might say that, contrary to its rival on the other bank, this is still a real *route*, not just a functional means of communication but a sort of complex *experience* in which occur simultaneously a continuous spectacle (the Adour is a very beautiful, unappreciated river) and the memory of an ancestral practice, that of walking, of the slow and rhythmic penetration of the landscape, which then assumes different proportions; here you return to what I was saying earlier, which is basically the power this country has of evading the immobility of postcards: don't try too hard to take photographs: to judge, to love it, you must come and stay, so that you can savor the variegation of sites, seasons, weather, and light.

SOMEONE WILL SAY: all you talk about are things like the weather, vaguely esthetic or in any case purely subjective impressions. But the people, their relations, industries, commerce, problems . . . ? Even though you're just a resident, don't you see any of that?—I enter these regions of reality in my fashion, that is, with my body; and my body is my childhood, as history has made it. This history has given me a provincial, meridional, bourgeois youth. For me, these three components are indistinct; for me, the bourgeoisie is the provinces, and the provinces are Bayonne; the countryside (of my childhood) is always the Bayonnais hinterland, a network of excursions, visits, and stories. Hence, at the age when memory is formed, I acquired of those "realities" only the *sensation* they afforded me: odors, exhaustions, sounds of voices, errands, changing light, everything that, with regard to reality, is somehow irresponsible and having no meaning except to form, later on, the memory of lost time (entirely different from my Parisian childhood: filled with material difficulties, that childhood had, you might say, the harsh abstraction of poverty, and of the Paris of that period I have virtually no "impressions"). If I speak of this Sud-Ouest as memory refracts it within me, it is because I trust Joubert's formula: "Do not express yourself as you feel, but as you remember."

These inconsequentialities, then, are a kind of gateway to that huge region with which sociological data and political analysis are concerned. Nothing, for instance, has more importance in my memory than the odors of that old neighborhood, between Nive and Adour, which is called *le petit Bayonne*: all the objects of petty commerce mingled there to constitute an inimitable fragrance: the string for making sandals (here the word "espadrilles" is not used) braided by old Basque men, hot chocolate, Spanish olive oil, the congested look of the dark shops and the narrow streets, the flyspecked paper of the books in the municipal library—it all functioned like the chemical formula of a vanished commerce (though this neighborhood still keeps a little of the old charm), or, more exactly, functions today like the formula of that disappearance. By its smell I can detect the actual change of a certain type of consumption: the sandals (soles pathetically lined with rubber) are no longer handmade, the chocolate and the olive oil are bought outside the town, in a supermarket. The odors are over and done with—as if, paradoxically, the increase in urban pollution drove off the household smells, as if "purity" were a perfidious form of pollution.

A further induction: in my childhood I knew many families of the Bayonnais bourgeoisie (there was something quite Balzacian about the Bayonne of those days); I knew their habits, their rituals, their conversations, their way of life. That liberal bourgeoisie was chock full of prejudices, not of assets; there was a kind of distortion between the ideology of that class (frankly reactionary) and its economic status (sometimes tragic). Such distortion is never accounted for by sociological or political analysis, which functions as a very coarse filter and loses the "subtleties" of the social dialectic. Now, these subtleties—or these paradoxes of History—even if I could not formulate them, I felt them: I was already "reading" the Sud-Ouest, I covered the text that proceeds from the light of a landscape, from the languor of a day oppressed by the wind from Spain, to a whole type of discourse, social and provincial. For "to read" a country is first of all to perceive it in terms of the body and of memory, in terms of the body's memory. I believe it is to this vestibule of knowledge and of analysis that the writer is assigned: more conscious than competent, conscious of the very interstices of competence. That is why childhood is the royal road by which we know a country best. Ultimately, there is no Country but childhood's.

L'Humanité, 1977

INCIDENTS

In Morocco, not long ago . . .

(

THE BARTENDER, in a station restaurant, came out to pick a red geranium and put it in a glass of water, between the coffee machine and the sink full of dirty cups and saucers.

(

In the square in front of the Socco, his blue shirttails flying, an emblem of Disorder, a furious boy (which in this country means a boy with all the features of madness) gesticulates and rails at a European (*Go home!*). Then vanishes. A few seconds later, the sound of chanting indicates the approach of a funeral; the procession appears. Among the bearers (in relays) of the coffin, the same boy, temporarily subdued.

(

Heard the King's Cousin, who is very dark, pass himself off as an American Negro (pretending not to know Arabic).

(

Tonsorial persecution: Rafaelito claims his father cut his hair off while he was asleep. Other boys say that the police crop them whenever they can catch them in the street: rebellion and repression on the level of the boys' black hair.

(

Two elderly American women seize the elbows of a tall blind man even older than themselves and walk him across the street between them. But what he wanted, this Oedipus, was money: money, money, not assistance.

(

A delicate, almost gentle, boy, his hands already a little coarse, suddenly makes the triggerlike gesture that reveals the young punk: flicking the ash off his cigarette with the back of a fingernail.

(

Abder asks for a clean towel, which, out of a religious fear of contamination, must be kept here beside the bed, to purify himself afterward of love.

(

A venerable hadji with a neatly trimmed short gray beard and carefully manicured hands, artistically draped in a snow-white djellaba of extremely fine cloth, drinking a glass of milk.

Yet this: a stain, a faint smear of something, maybe pigeon shit, on his immaculate hood.

(

A European woman, no longer young, heavily made up, filthy, preposterously swathed in whatever sways and frays, hair in braids, fringes on cloak, bag, and skirts, passes through the Socco. This Pendulous Wonder (I am told by a boy who doesn't bat an eye) is a "Soviet witch."

(

The child I find in the corridor was sleeping in an old cardboard box, his head sticking out as though cut off.

(

Near the Socco, a European couple has set up shop, selling fast food for hippies. A sign says: *Hygiene is our specialty.* And the woman empties her ashtray in the street—which is not *British*.

(

A young girl is punished in public by her mother, a peasant woman. The daughter screams. The mother is calm, persistent; she has seized the girl's hair as if it were a swatch of cloth and proceeds to deliver a series of regular blows to her head. A circle forms instantly. The masseur's judgment: the mother is right. —Why? —The girl is a whore (as a matter of fact, he knows nothing about her).

15

(

The child—he can't be more than five—in shorts, and a hat: knocks on a door—spits—adjusts his crotch.

(

An old blind beggar with a white beard, wearing a djellaba: magisterial, impassive, classical, theatrical, Sophoclean, while the face of the adolescent boy who begs for him assumes the whole expressive burden that such a situation allows: agonized features contorted by a glowering pout display suffering, poverty, injustice, doom: Look! look! the child's face says, look at this man who can no longer see.

(

The little girls illicitly peddling mint, lemon (Virgil). The vile plainclothes cop looks very tough; he abuses them, brutalizes them, but lets them run away.

(

Delicious fantasy: a certain Mohammed with soft hands, who works in the textile factory, insists that the Jews' mosque is dark on Saturdays; he points it out to me: it is the church of the Spanish Capuchins; the Jews, he says, use it (it has been lent to them) for their services.

(

An adolescent black, in a wretched raincoat and a bright blue sombrero, and a hippie girl, barefoot on the filthy sidewalk, pass in front of the natives of the Café Central: the boy has picked up a girl but publicly sacrifices to an insane Westernism.

(

The Iberia official does not smile. She has a peremptory voice, heavy (but dry) makeup, very long bloodred nails— these nails shuffle the long tickets, folding them with a practiced and authoritative gesture . . .

(

A pot for mint tea, made of hammered metal without a plastic stopper, bought with the help of the middleweight boxing champion of Morocco.

(

Since I had the foresight to inform the King's Cousin I would be quite useless to him, he reassures me: I could advise him about investing the millions he plans to make from his gin distillery.

(

Abdessalam, a boarder at Tétouan, seems to have come to Tangiers this morning (our meeting entirely accidental) to buy an antirheumatism salve and a whistling stopper for his kettle.

❨

A young black, crème-de-menthe shirt, almond-green pants, orange socks, and apparently very soft red shoes.

❨

Watching a bearded man dancing, the King's Cousin informs me that this is a philosopher. In order to be a philosopher, he says, four things are necessary: (1) to have a certificate in Arabic; (2) to travel a great deal; (3) to have contacts with other philosophers; (4) to be remote from reality, for example at the seaside.

❨

A young black who looks as though he were powdered with white, in a Day-Glo parka.

❨

At the Socco, in July, the terrace is full of people. A group of hippies takes a table, one couple among them; the husband is a plump blond fellow wearing nothing under his overalls; the wife is in a long Wagnerian nightgown; she holds the hand of a tiny limp white girl whom she encourages to shit on the sidewalk, between the legs of her companions who do not react.

❨

Vain attempt to find a blue djellaba. Siri's comment: there are no blue sheep.

C

Mustafa is in love with his cap. He won't take it off to make love.

C

In the patio of the Hotel Minzah, a rather haggard woman in a long red dress gives me a sharp look and asks for "les cabinets."

C

A demonstration of phonological pertinence: a young vendor in the bazaar (with an appealing glance):
tu/*ti* (you/yuh: non-pertinent) *veux tapis*/*taper* (want a rug/want to fuck: pertinent)?

C

Aliwa (a good name to repeat over and over) likes immaculate white trousers (late in the season), but the toilets being what they are, there is always a stain on these milk-white garments.

C

On the beach at Tangiers (families, fags, boys), some old workmen, like very slow, very ancient insects, rake the sand.

C

Selam, a veteran from Tangiers, bursts out laughing because he has met three Italians who were of no use to him: "They thought I was feminine!"

(

An old peasant in a brown djellaba (the deep color of rags) carries over his shoulder a huge braid of old-rose Spanish onions.

(

"Papa," a charming and crazy old Englishman, *in sympathy* gives up his lunch during Ramadan (*in sympathy* for the circumcised little boys).

(

At nine in the morning, a fierce young fellow walks through the Socco, a live sheep over his shoulders, hooves tied in front (a pastoral and biblical attitude). A little girl passes, caressing a hen in her arms.

(

Through the hotel window, on the rather deserted promenade (it is still early on Sunday morning: in the distance, boys are going to the beach to play ball), I see a sheep and a little fantailed dog; the sheep follows right on the dog's heels; finally he tries to mount him.

(

From the train he has just left at a deserted station (Asilah), I watched him run down the road, alone in the rain, hugging the empty cigar box he had asked me to give him "to keep his papers in."

☾

In a street of Salé, someone says there's going to be a police raid, everyone in rags makes a getaway. A boy of fourteen is sitting there, a tray of old pastry in his lap. A huge military policeman heads straight for him, knees him in the belly, and snatches the tray, without stopping or turning around, without a word (the police will certainly eat the pastry). The boy's face is contorted, but he manages not to cry; he hesitates, then vanishes. —The presence of two friends embarrasses me and keeps me from giving him two thousand francs.

☾

A Racinian opening: with a gentle willingness: "You see me? Do you want to touch me?"

☾

A good-looking young man, well dressed in a gray suit and wearing a gold bracelet, his hands delicate and clean, smoking a pack of red Olympics, drinking tea, speaking quite intensely (some sort of official? the kind that checks the dossiers?), drools a tiny thread of saliva onto his knee; his companion points this out to him.

☾

He energetically cleans the bidet with the little washroom broom. When I remark on this: "Only for the bidet!"

21

(

At a concert (German, of course), two young Arabs talking very seriously in the lobby (realizing they are being watched and therefore, in European fashion, not looking back); one, in a corduroy jacket, with a pipe in his mouth.

(

In a restaurant in Rabat, four men from the country—among sauces, salads, meats, and three-button suits—drink sugared milk and slowly chew bread torn off a huge loaf.

(

A certain Ahmed, near the station, wears a sky-blue sweater with a fine orange stain on the front.

(

A crowd, actually a mob, in the distance placards, banners, police whistles. A strike, a political demonstration? No, a pathetic initiation ceremony of the Mohammedia School of Engineering: a girl in a miniskirt on a truck, French songs, edifying slogans: "We Know We Have Work to Do," "Freshmen Today, Engineers Tomorrow."

(

Farid, encountered at Jour et Nuit, curses out a beggar who first asks me for a cigarette, then, having gotten it, for money "so I can eat." This gradual scheme of exploitation (though banal enough) seems to outrage Farid: "That's how he thanks you for having given him something!" Then, a minute later, as I leave him, giving him my whole pack of cigarettes, which he pockets without a word of thanks, I hear him asking me for five thousand francs "so I can eat." When I burst out laughing, he alleges the *difference* (here everyone asserts himself as different, because he conceives himself not as a person but as a need).

C

Abdellatif—a voluptuous boy—peremptorily justifies the Baghdad hangings. The guilt of the accused is obvious, since the trial went so fast: the case was clear. Contradiction between the brutality of this nonsense and the fresh warmth of his body, the availability of his hands, which I continue, somewhat dazed, to hold and to caress while he pours out his vengeful catechism.

C

Visit from an unknown boy, sent by his friend: "What do you want? Why are you here?" —"It's nature!" (Another boy, on another occasion: "It's love!")

C

Chella park: a tall youth with straight hair, dressed all in white, ankle boots under the white jeans, accompanied by his two veiled sisters, stares hard at me and spits: rejection or contingency?

(

Hard to bring back from Paris a "souvenir" for this boy who had asked me for one: What sort of pleasant trifle can you give someone who is totally indigent? A lighter?—to light what cigarettes? I opt for a coded, in other words, excessively useless, souvenir: a brass Eiffel Tower.

(

A Frenchman, a derelict of the Protectorate (hardware store), aphasic (rifle butt in the face, he stammers painfully), but ataxic as well, slowly digging up two wicks for my butane lamp, suddenly finds a loud, clear voice to scream at his dog (which has done nothing but be there), twice over: *Damn bitch!*

(

Driss A. doesn't know that sperm is called sperm—he calls it shit: "Watch out, the shit's going to come now": nothing more traumatizing.

Another boy, Slaui (Mohammed Gymnastique), says dryly and precisely: *ejaculate*: "Watch out, I'm going to ejaculate."

(

Going downstairs, I hand Mustafa (charming, smiling, ardent, honest) my sandals to carry, while I get out my key ("Here, hold this"). Later I realize he has kept them (suppression of the loan).

C

At the bank: a blind beggar staggers in, his cane fumbling around doors, counters, tellers' windows. A customer gives him a coin. The teller: "Don't do that, you'll get them in the habit."

C

At Jour et Nuit, a shoeshine boy: splendid eyes and smile, diligent. His name is Driuish (little dervish). Leaving, already some distance away, he gives me a friendly wave.

C

Lahucine, at the house. He is sitting opposite me, inert, placid, all morning. Never have hands been in such repose: only a painter could show it. In his presence, I am excessively active: constantly doing something, continually changing whatever it is I do: writing, reading a newspaper, sharpening a pencil, putting on another record, etc.

C

Mulay, the building super, lets me know with an imperious gesture that while I am away his young wife Aisha, to safeguard the apartment against "thieves," will sleep on the floor, here in the doorway, on the matting near the couch (tiny piece of matting, the size of a bathmat on the tiles).

(

The young *pied-noir*, a reconstructed petit bourgeois, wears his sweater draped over his shoulders, the sleeves knotted in front; he drops his car keys on the café table; his accent is harsh and quick, as though abruptly twisted off.

(

Two law students:
One, Abdellatif (French law), Westernized, two years in Switzerland (apparently), elegant (blue pullover, expensive beige corduroy suit), refined accent, a liar (says he's in second year, which I know to be false), gives me the Boredom routine (getting out of this country) and asks this question: What do you think of Pompidou?"
The other, Najib, encountered the next day in the same place, thus replacing the first boy, a student of Arab law, naturally elegant but poorly dressed (white T-shirt, heavy brown corduroys, worn shoes with buckles), with warm eyes, cool delicate hands, not dramatizing his boredom, says his vocation is *to become a minister*. He asks me to explain whether ministers, changing posts, are specialized, specifically trained or not (no critical intention).

(

The Trésorerie générale, a fortress-bank in the French style, is continuously surrounded by a horde of cripples, hopping around like sparrows on a lump of dung: one legless fellow, apparently the bicycle guard, bears down vehemently on a wretched client . . .

‹

Amid the group's rather lascivious horseplay, one of the *lycée* boys brings up the latest theme assignment: "Compare the pedagogy of Rabelais with that of Montaigne."

‹

According to his schoolmates, H. is "very sensual" (a phrase made all the more disturbing by the dryness of the *pied-noir* accent): in my mind, it becomes H.'s name: Very Sensual. Yet the nickname's meaning is easy enough to guess: H. lets himself be fucked.

‹

"I'm afraid I'm falling in love with you. It's a problem. What should I do?"
"Give me your address."

‹

While little Mohammed recites the verses he has just composed (unless they're by Sully Prudhomme), I keep thinking how lucky it is that I've met him, since I'll ask him to go buy me a couple of pounds of tomatoes at the neighborhood grocery.

‹

Amal seems enchanted by his own name: he tells it to me right away, fatuously providing the translation ("My name is Hope," he says), delighted whenever the word appears in a song.

(

Mohammed (of course), a policeman's son, wants (later on, when he's through with the *lycée*), to be a police inspector: that's his vocation. Moreover (he says): he likes football (right guard), pinball, and girls.

(

Though the shop window is crammed with the latest kinds of electronic equipment, the two salesmen whom I ask for a cassette player can't sell me one. The younger man doesn't know how to operate the machine he shows me: a whole series of buttons pressed with absurd results: lid flying open, batteries reversed, painful noises, and no music. The other man, the boss, busy with something or other, sulky, shows no interest and immediately decides that it's the machine that is defective. All of which is not much encouragement to buy a machine for eighty thousand francs.

(

Mohammed L., encountered one morning around ten, is still half-asleep; he just got up, he says, because last night he composed some verses for a play he's writing—"no characters, no plot," etc.—and stayed up very late. Another Mohammed, the little one, told me he wrote poetry "to keep from being bored." In this country poetry allows you *to go to bed too late.*

(

Amidou, second-year student, future gym teacher, encountered one Sunday morning in the dust of the flea market, poor and good-natured, his raincoat too short, his big shoes coming apart, his fine Moroccan eyes, his kinky hair, has to "reflect" for tomorrow on "Molière's notion of comedy."

Amidou: I prefer spelling my name without an *h*, since:
Doux comme l'amidon (smooth as paste)
Inflammable comme l'amadou (inflammable as tinder).

(

I enjoy Amidou's vocabulary: *dream* and *burst* for *get an erection* and *have an orgasm*. *Burst* is vegetal, scattering, disseminating, not moralistic, narcissistic, closed off.

(

Ramadan: the moon will soon be up. We have to wait another half hour to make love: "I'm starting to dream." "Is that allowed?" "I don't know."

(

A., leaving the other day after having "dreamed," came in his underwear once he was out in the street; but he couldn't wash himself off, as his religion prescribes, because his boarding school grants only one shower every eight days, etc. (resentment transferred to the State).

(

Sitting on the balcony, they wait for the tiny red lamp to be lit on the tip of the minaret, marking the end of the fast.

(

Every afternoon of Ramadan, around five (this is November), the Restaurant de la Libération, in the medina, seen from the street, is transformed into a hospice with long rows of tables where the men line up to eat their soup; the sole waiter on duty runs back and forth, like a lay brother.

(

Naciri knows French well; to prove it, he studs his discourse with foreign phrases: "Ils sont sortis ce soir, *because Ramadan.*"

(

The "head bookkeeper" (a boy with an attractive face) pronounces solemnly: "Civilization is when you know your rights and are conscious of your duties." After which, like the rest of us, he bursts out laughing.

(

This Friday evening, when Ramadan ends, there is still no smoking, because when we walk off the street into a Jewish house, the Sabbath is beginning.

(

French professors discussing a doctoral candidate: what teaching skills has he shown? Confusion, embarrassment. Suddenly, to the great relief of all, someone exclaims: his *agrégation* lecture!

(

Tonsorials: my shoeshine boy, bending over my feet, reveals the huge bald spot on the back of his skull, while behind him, on the sidewalk, a boy in rags obsessively rakes
his close-cropped dusty hair with a toy comb.

(

Relation between his very delicate, carefully groomed
hands (he had just washed them) and the way in which he
showed them, played with them, incorporated them, as he
talked, into the *pied-noir*'s gesture repertory. Relation between the extreme delicacy of his expensive black socks and
his way of stretching his legs.

(

A clumsy, half-mad shoeshine boy always hurls himself
on me, insistently offering: "Me, shine, Chinese" (the ad-
jective of perfection).

(

The same day:
on the one hand, the petit bourgeois student stupidly
showing off for the others in order to "stick the prof," who
contradicts me with a statement so ridiculous that nothing
remains in it but the message of ill will;
on the other, Mustafa, called Musta: hair cropped, fine
almond-shaped eyes, an almost Roman head except for the
sweetness of his expression; born in Fez, he is eighteen and
too poor to continue his studies; looking for work in Rabat,

he has taken a job with a carpenter at Akkari; he earns thirty-five hundred francs a week. His father does nothing, his mother works in a textile factory. He lives with one of his sisters. A being devoid of any hostility.

C

A determined little Frenchwoman, whose puny lover is carrying huge suitcases, answers the ticket collector ("You've got quite a load there"): "They're such thieves, these porters, but they don't take us in for a moment." Good-natured laughter of the ticket taker, though he is as annoyed as the porters.

C

Young compatriots—with girls to show off for—pretending to speak English with an exaggerated French accent (a way of concealing the fact, without losing face, that they will never have a good accent).

C

Medina: at six in the evening, in the street studded with peddlers, one sad fellow offers a single chopping board on the edge of the sidewalk.

C

Behind me, on the plane, an old French lady, chatting with the woman beside her, is doing needlepoint: a grayish piece of buckram with old-fashioned bouquets drawn on it. Later, not getting off at the intermediate stop, she continues

her work during the landing and the takeoff, absolutely
static amid the plane's movements: imperturbable figure.

C

Two conductors, off duty, sitting at the bar; the younger
one hands a cup of coffee to the older man, who refuses with
a smile. Later, I realize that the older man is only an assis-
tant, he has only one star on his cap, the younger man has
three.

C

In the train, there are around me: (1) a woman traveling
alone, she has a Teutonic accent (Alsatian, Swiss?), wears a
ponytail with a scarf knotted around it; she tries to make
contact with me, accepts a lunch tray when I do, orders nothing to drink then wants *selzer* water, ice, etc.; she is reading
Rif, Terre de légendes; (2) a black Moroccan woman, pustular;
she wears a wine-colored caftan and high-button shoes and
holds a kinky-haired baby in her arms; (3) a modest *pied
noir* woman doing some kind of complicated crochet stitch;
(4) two lesbians playing cards; (5) a young Moroccan, barefoot.

C

Group taxi: a "député" from Tétouan (an architect, he
has built a whole street in Madrid, which has made him a
multimillionaire) directs through the dark and the rain our
old taxi driver (gray workshirt and yellow skullcap), who
sees nothing, by loud, abrupt, metallic interjections, the way

you drive an old carriage horse, moreover a perfectly docile one.

C

Azrou Workers' Cooperative: a flock of little girls huddled together like birds and cheeping over huge carpets hung in front of them: a mixture of aviary and classroom; from this to the Sadean seraglio.

C

At Ito, looking out over a huge, noble landscape, one of us jokingly gives a picture of a naked woman (from some *Playboy* or other) to young Moha, who sells semiprecious stones: smiles, reserve, seriousness, remoteness on the boy's part: he is the one who masters a scene initially intended to ridicule him; the other boy's hysteria remains here, *on the distaff side.*

C

Abdelkader, a boy with shining eyes and an imperious smile, endowed with an absolute friendliness, manifesting in all its glory, beyond any form of culture, the very essence of *charity*: no other word for it (Tinerhir).

C

Two hippie hitchhikers. *Ideology*: one of them talks to me about the "stream of consciousness." *Economy*: going to Marrakesh to buy Indian shirts, which they will sell at very high prices in Holland. *Ritual*: as soon as they are in the back of the car, they roll cigarettes and deliberately, mechanically plunge into absence (from which they awake as soon as they are offered a coffee).

C

But also: at Settat, I picked up a hitchhiker twelve years old; he carries a huge plastic bag filled with oranges, tangerines, and a package wrapped in filthy waxed paper; docile, serious, reserved, he sets none of this down, keeping it on his knees, in the hollow of his djellaba. His name is Abdellatif. Out in open country, without a village in sight, he tells me to stop and points to the plain: that's where he's going. He kisses my hand and gives me two dirhams (probably the bus fare, which he had got ready and was holding in his fist).

C

Savoir-vivre in Marrakesh: fleeting conversation from open carriage to bicycle: cigarette given, rendezvous made, the bicycle turns the corner and vanishes.

C

In the Rue Samarine, I was walking against the current of this human stream. I had the feeling (nothing erotic about it) that each one had a *ʒob* (Arab argot for penis) and that all these *ʒobs*, as I passed them, were lined up like a mass-produced object rhythmically stamped out by a mold. In this stream, but dressed in the same rough cloth, in the same colors, the same rags, from time to time, a *ʒob* missing.

(

Marrakesh souk: wild roses in the piles of mint.

(

The little Marrakesh schoolteacher: "I'll do whatever you want," he says, effusively, his eyes filled with kindness and complicity. Which means: *I'll fuck you*, and that's all.

(

A black man, entirely swathed and hooded in his white djellaba, thereby becomes so black that I take his face for a woman's *litham*.

(

On the road between Marrakesh and Beni-Mellal: a poor boy, Abdelkahaim, speaking no French, carries a round, rustic basket. I give him a lift for a few hundred yards. No sooner in the car than he takes a teapot out of his basket and hands me a glass of hot tea (how can it be hot?); then he gets out, vanishes at the roadside.

(

A very poor hitchhiker moving from town to town looking for work (very nice eyes) tells me a grim story of a group taxi (we're driving through a sort of woods) whose driver was murdered by four passengers disguised as women. "But those jitney drivers never have much money." "It doesn't matter: a thief's a thief."

(

"Monsieur, remember, you should never give a lift to a Moroccan you don't know," says this Moroccan to whom I'm giving a lift and whom I don't know.

(

A girl begging: "My father's dead. It's to buy a notebook," etc. (The nasty part of mendicancy is the tedium of the stereotypes.)

(

On the road between Agadir and Tamri, a person in some sort of uniform: civilian, filthy, ragged, but an official's cap and a revolver holster: he is a forest ranger. He likes detective stories, because "he too, in a way, is a kind of detective (keeps an eye on the thefts of wood); he occasionally finds himself confronting similar problems," etc.

(

The Moroccan student, with slightly buck teeth and a little beard, has a Catholic scholarship from Lille, because there was a white father in his Upper Atlas village. He is reading (or not reading) *Les Fleurs du mal.*

(

Front legs tied and folded, forced to kneel as though in abasement, a camel makes terrible efforts to get up. Another, crouching on the ground, immobilized, bleeding from the mouth, exhibited as though in the stocks, a circle of spectators standing around it (including tourists, one potbellied and pink, in tight shorts, camera slung over one shoulder), the camel meanwhile shrieking horribly, kicking *with all its might*. His master, a small black man, beats him, picks up a handful of sand and throws it in his eyes.

(

Gérard, whose father is French and whose mother is a native woman, wants to show me the way to the Gazelle d'Or; he sprawls in the car in order to reveal his charms; then, as a rare delicacy, a final, irresistible argument: "You know, my thing, it's not cut!"

(

Three young Chleuhs, on the cliff, ask for a French lesson. "How do you say . . . ?" Answering them, I realize that the sexual organ preserves a consonantal paradigm: *cul/con/queue*. The three young fellows, instant philologists, are amazed.

(

A boy sitting on a low wall, at the side of the road, which he ignores—sitting there as though for eternity, sitting there in order to be sitting, *without equivocation*:
"Seated peaceably, doing nothing,
Spring comes and the grass grows of its own accord."

(

A certain Jean, a young professor—of what?—leans over my book: "I could never get that guy (Proust) through my head; but I feel it'll happen one of these days." His friend Pierre, dumbfounded, disdainful, and dry (indifferent to the answer): "Are you taking notes?"

(

Azemur: bought a tin tureen from a young and toothless vendor who offers to meet me "in his *garçonnière*."

(

Happiness at Mehiula: the huge kitchen, at night, the storm outside, the simmering *harrira*, the big butane lamps, the whole ballet of little visits, the warmth, the djellaba, and reading Lacan! (Lacan defeated by this trivial comfort.)

(

The marabout guardian is a toothless old woman who initiates the village boys for fifty francs apiece.

(The tomb is near a mud cube marked with the number 61—this is the room where the dead are washed; the grave is open: some mats on the ground, cloths hung as gifts on the green-painted wooden coffin under a faded photo of the former sultan, a pair of sandals abandoned on a mat.)

(

M., sick, huddled in a corner on a mat, concealed his bare and burning feet under his brown djellaba.

‹

A big, toothless lout of a fellow, his tone convinced and passionate, whispers about the most ordinary brand of cigarettes: "Marquise: for me, it's as good as kif!"

‹

Little I. brings me flowers, a real country bouquet: a few heads of geranium, a spray of red briar roses, two roses, four sprigs of jasmine. He has had this impulse after the great pleasure I have given him: typing his name several different ways on a piece of paper that I presented him (flowers in exchange for writing).

Having given one of them an aspirin, now they all have headaches and I become a dispensary.

‹

A group of boys chipped in to pay for a whore; one bicycled thirty kilometers to find her in A., and to bring back something to drink; then each took his turn.

‹

This country: where even Boy Scouts can be reprehensible. I give three of them a lift to town: rather shabby, long hair uncombed, caps of all kinds—and yet a flag, badges, Scout salute, phraseology ("Scouts are everyone's brother"). Bare-legged, the "master" sported an erection, while the others were singing sad Scout songs (story of an orphan).

❨

Over the door, in the cement, the mason Ahmed Midace has engraved these words in clumsy letters: CUISINE PAR FORCE. The father didn't want this extra kitchen, the mother did.

❨

Two naked boys have slowly crossed the wadi, their clothes in bundles on their heads.

❨

The peace of a djellaba (from behind) on a donkey, the sign regularly repeated in the countryside.

(1969)

AT LE PALACE
TONIGHT...

◖

I CONFESS I AM unable to interest myself in the beauty of
a place if there are no people in it (I don't like empty
museums); and conversely, in order to discover the interest
of a face, of a figure, of a garment, to savor the encounter,
I require that the site of this discovery have its interest and
its savor as well. Which may be why Le Palace beguiles me.
I feel relaxed there. It's modern—even very modern? Yet I
recognize here the old power of authentic architecture,
which is conjointly to enhance the moving, dancing bodies,
and to animate the spaces and the structures.

These days, theaters die easily. The hall where I saw my
first Beckett is now a garage; others become movie houses,
give way to apartments. Le Palace is a rescued theater; first
of all because shows will be given here; then because, from
the theater it originally was (and several times over), everything has been preserved: stage, curtain, balcony, orchestra
(transformed into a splendid dance floor, but from which
you can see the show, standing or sitting on cushions), the
great swathes of red velvet: inveterate emotion: to climb a
staircase and emerge into a huge space, crisscrossed with
lights and shadows, suddenly to enter, like an initiate, the

sacred space of representation (even and especially when, as here, the show is throughout the entire hall). *Theater*: this Greek word comes from a verb that means "to see." Le Palace is certainly a site dedicated to looking: you spend your time looking at the hall; and, when you come back from the dancing, you look some more.

Le Palace is well proportioned. This means that *you are not afraid here* (you would not mind sleeping in it): too small, a theater is stifling; too big, chilling. Here you can circulate—up, down, changing places according to your whim— a freedom always frustrated in other theaters, where everyone is assigned a seat, the one corresponding to his money. Yet freedom is not enough to make a good space. Certain experiments have shown that the little white mouse suffers great anxiety when placed in an empty arena lacking any point of reference. To feel comfortable in a space, I must in fact be able to proceed from one reference point to another, to inhabit a corner as well as a platform, and, like Robinson happy on his island, to make my way in comfort from one domicile to the next. At Le Palace, the familiar places are many: a salon for chatting, bars to meet in, to rest in between dances, a belvedere from which to gaze, above the intervals of the balustrades, down at the immense spectacle of lights playing over bodies. From each place where I take up my position, I have the delightful impression of occupying a sort of imperial box, from which I can master all that happens.

Is not the great raw material of modern art, of our daily art—is it not, in this era, light? In ordinary theaters, light is remote, fastened to the stage. At Le Palace, it is the whole theater that is the stage; here light occupies a deep space, within which it comes alive and performs like an actor; an intelligent laser, with a complicated and refined mind, like an exhibitor of abstract sculptures, produces enigmatic traces, with sudden mutations: circles, rectangles, ellipses, tracks, cables, galaxies, fringes. The remarkable thing is not the technological prowess (though that is rare enough in Paris), but the appearance of a new art, in its material (a mobile light) and in its practice; for this is actually a public art, in that it is achieved among the public and not in front of it, and a total art (the old Greek and Wagnerian dream), where scintillation, music, and desire unite. This means that "art," without breaking with past culture (the sculpture of space by laser may indeed recall certain plastic efforts of modernity), extends beyond the constraints of cultural training: a liberation confirmed by a new mode of consumption: we look at the lights, the shadows, the settings, but also we do something else at the same time (we dance, we talk, we look at each other): a practice known to the ancient theater.

At Le Palace, I am not obliged to dance in order to sustain a living relationship with this site. Alone, or at least somewhat apart, I can "dream." In this humanized space, I can exclaim to myself now and then: "How strange all this is!" Strange, the old stage curtain, where I read an advertisement for *la French Line*: Le Havre-Plymouth-New York (bizarre: in this chain of places, it is Plymouth that sets me dreaming: perhaps the romantic myth of the port of call?). Strange, the dark dancers (backlighting) in the mist that momentarily covers the floor, articulated like puppets under a ceiling of red and green rays. Strange, the revolving mirror. Strange, the sooty, Hellenoid frescoes that run like a slightly dated chastity along the upper walls.

Le Palace is not a *boîte*, a "box," as we French call a nightclub: it collects in an original site pleasures ordinarily dispersed: that of the theater as an edifice lovingly preserved, the pleasure of what is seen; the excitement of the Modern, the exploration of new visual sensations, due to new technologies; the delight of the dance, the charm of possible meetings. All this combined creates something very old, which is called *la Fête* and which is quite different from Amusement or Distraction: a whole apparatus of sensations destined to make people happy, for the interval of a night. What is new is this impression of synthesis, of totality, of complexity: I am in a place sufficient unto itself. It is by this supplement that Le Palace is not a simple enterprise but *a work*, and that those who conceived it may regard themselves with good reason as artists.

Would Proust have liked it? I don't know: there are no duchesses anymore. Yet, leaning down over the dance floor of Le Palace throbbing with colored beams and dancing silhouettes, divining around me in the shadow of levels and of open loges an entire ebullition of young bodies busy in their unsuspected circuits, I seemed to recognize, transposed to the modern, something I had read in Proust: that evening at the Opéra, where the house and the boxes form, under the young Narrator's impassioned eye, an aquatic milieu, gently illuminated by aigrettes, by glances, by jewels, by faces, by gestures suggestive of those made by undersea deities, amid which sat enthroned the duchess of Guermantes. Nothing but a metaphor after all, traveling from far back in my memory and arriving to embellish Le Palace with a final charm: the one that comes to us from the fictions of culture.

Vogue-Hommes, MAY 1978

SOIRÉES DE PARIS

☾

So, we're well out of it.

SCHOPENHAUER
(on a loose sheet, before dying)

24 AUGUST 1979

Lᴀsᴛ ɴɪɢʜᴛ.) At the Flore where I read *Le Monde* (no news), beside me two boys (I know one of them by sight and we even nod to each other; nice looking, regular features, but coarse fingernails) have a long argument about telephone wake-up service: it rings twice, but if you don't wake up by then, you're out of luck; all this now by computer, etc. In the Métro, quite full, it seemed to me, of young foreigners (perhaps from the Gare du Nord and the Gare de l'Est), a guitarist (American folk songs) passing the hat in one car; I carefully chose the next car, but at Odéon he changed cars and got in mine (he probably works the whole train); seeing which, I got right off and returned to the car he had just left (passing the hat always embarrasses me as a form of hysteria and blackmail, and an arrogance as well, as if it was self-evident that such music or any music always gives me pleasure). I got off at Strasbourg-Saint-Denis, the station echoing to a saxophone solo; at the bend of a corridor I noticed a thin young black producing this enormous, "inconsiderate" noise. *Run-down* character of the neighbor-

51

hood. I took the Rue d'Aboukir, thinking of Charlus, who
mentions it; I didn't know it came out so close to the Bou-
levards. It was not yet eight-thirty; I delayed a little so as
not to turn up exactly on time at 104, where Patricia L.
would have to come down to let me in. The neighborhood
was deserted, dirty, a strong wind was blowing, raising huge
piles of papers and empty boxes, the detritus of the factories
of this neighborhood; I discovered a tiny triangular square
(Rue d'Alexandrie, I think); it was charming and sordid,
three old plane trees (I sympathized with their lack of air),
some oddly shaped benches that looked like tubs, and along
one side a low, bright-painted building—I thought it might
be a tiny, very shabby music hall but no, it was another box
factory; beside it, on a patch of wall, a huge movie poster
(Peter Ustinov flanked by two young women); I went on to
the Rue Saint-Denis; but there were so many prostitutes you
couldn't really "stroll" here without seeming to be doing
something else; I retraced my steps, it was boring, no shop
windows to look at, and I sat down for a minute on one of
the benches of the little square; some kids were playing football and shouting; others were flinging themselves on top
of huge piles of paper that the wind was beginning to scatter.
I thought: how much like a movie! I ought to shoot this to
get it into a film; I fantasized a little, imagining one tech-
nique that would allow me to film the scene immediately (a
perfect camera where my second shirtbutton is), and another
that would make this square with the wind blowing through
it a setting where you could put a character after the fact.
Finally I went to 104, still musing, alarmed by the grim
power of this corner of Paris, passing in front of the hotel
Royal-Aboukir (what a name!). All this was like some dis-

inherited New York neighborhood, on the smaller Parisian scale. At dinner (a good risotto, but the beef, of course, not cooked at all), I felt comfortable with friends: A. C., Philippe Roger, Patricia, and a young woman, Frédérique, who was wearing a rather formal gown, its unusual shade of blue soothing; she didn't say much, but she was *there*, and I thought that such attentive and marginal presences were necessary to the good economy of a party (André T. exaggerates, though). They talked about what they called "shaggy-dog stories" ("At Victoria Station, in England, I met a Spanish girl who spoke French"), arguing excitedly over the definition of the concept; and about Khomeini (I said how much I regretted having only news bulletins these days, never analyses; no one tells us, for instance, what's happening to the class conflict in Iran, missing, on this point, Marx), then about Napoleon (because I happen to be reading Chateaubriand). I left first, around eleven-thirty, very eager to take a piss and, afraid I'd never find a taxi and would have to take the Métro, I went into a Boulevard bistro opposite the Porte Saint-Denis; in a corner, huddled near the toilet door which I could scarcely open, three indefinable creatures (half-pimps, half-queens) talking about a whore from Marseille (as far as I could make out); a handsome tattooed Asian (I saw the blue-green tattoos below the short sleeves of his T-shirt) was standing at the pinball machine with a friend. The barman and the proprietress, vulgar, tired, kindly: I thought, what a job! The taxi stank of dirt and some sort of pharmaceutical smell—yet the no-smoking sign was explicit. In bed, while Germaine Tailleferre eagerly propounded her platitudes and vanities in a voice and a diction I love, waiting impatiently for the Stravinsky and Satie records to end so that I could hear more of her—in bed, then, I glanced at the first pages of a text *M/S*, just published by Seuil (F. W. had told me about it), wondering what I could say and finding—though it was nicely written and sympathetic—no more than "yeah, yeah," then I continued, fascinated, with the history of Napoleon in *Mémoires d'outre-tombe*. After turning out the light, I went back to the radio for a while: a sour, fragile soprano doing an insipid classical aria (something like Campra, they're all alike), I turned it off.

25 AUGUST 1979

At the Flore with Eric M., we order soft-boiled eggs and sausages, and a glass of bordeaux. No one to look at. A gray-haired, bearded Argentinian comes to my table and renews an invitation he says he has already made to come, all expenses paid, to his Communications Institute; since I am evasive, he suddenly adds something like: "We are politically quite independent" (I wasn't thinking of that, but rather of the boredom of having to get through several dinners with him in Buenos Aires—we had to communicate in English). A young boy came in and sat down alone; impossible to determine his nationality (only the almond-shaped eyes are foreign); his close-fitting jacket is dark, formal, his collar rumpled over a thin tightly knotted tie, the outfit finished off (or begun?) by peculiar red buckskin shoes. The vendor of *Charlie-Hebdo* passes through; on the cover, in the stupid taste of that paper, a basket of greenish heads like lettuces: "2 Francs a Cambodian Head"; and just then a young Cambodian bustles into the café, sees the drawing, evidently shocked, disturbed, buys the paper: Cambodian heads! During all this, Eric and I discuss the question of diaries; I tell him I want to dedicate to him the text I have just written for *Tel Quel*, and his spontaneous pleasure touches me (the evening's recompense). He walks me home through the Rue de Rennes, amazed at the density of the hustlers, their beauty (I have more reservations), tells me he was hurt by Y., who has told him that P. put him down (a network incident, in Y.'s manipulative manner). In bed, to the music of the *Nutcracker* (broadcast to illustrate the notion of "musical fantasy"!), I read a little more of the latest Yves Navarre (better than the others) and *M/S* ("yeah, yeah"); but these seem like chores and as soon as some of my obligations are fulfilled I put them aside and turn with relief to Chateaubriand, the real book. Always this notion: suppose the Moderns were wrong? What if they had no talent?

26 AUGUST 1979

At the Bonaparte, where I am to meet Claude J. for dinner, Gérard L. finds me (I loathe these impromptu meetings, I prefer being alone in a café to look around, to think about my work, etc.): he is more down-and-out than ever; incoherent, gabbling, smiling gently under his curly hair and his blue eyes (either myopic or astonished behind his round spectacles), he reports that he has given up his room to share the apartment of *this guy*, in hopes of having a place to paint while the École des Beaux-Arts is closed (for the summer);

now it appears that this guy is crazy, making life impossible for both of them. How old is this guy? Twenty-four, a painter. Does he cruise you? No, that's just it (as if that was what was bothering G.L.), he's crazy, etc. I feel he is so absolutely incoherent, so absolutely and unconditionally needy, that it's exciting, like having a slave at one's disposal, and such confusion touches me, realizing what joy, what relief he would have if I were suddenly to say to him: *all right, then, come to my place.* I do nothing of the kind, it would be crazy. — Claude J. arrives, wearing a sweater; it is raining hard now, and cold. We hesitate over the restaurant, interminably; he generously offers me the choice of where to go, but such freedom is like an overwhelming present, I don't know what to do with it; he mentions a "meat place" near the Collège de France; even though the notion revolts me and I'm afraid it will be packed (which I loathe in restaurants), I'm so tired of walking in the rain that I prefer a restaurant some distance away (so we'll have to take his car); luckily the meat place is closed, so there's no choice but to go to Bofinger (which is really what I wanted to do from the start, being quite taken these days with this brasserie, which is excellent but expensive). The headwaiter calls me by my name, which I find flattering and embarrassing; the watercress salad is excellent and there is (something I've come to love, since my first trips to Italy) steamed fish and vegetables which I sprinkle with vinaigrette. Claude J. tells me about his trip to Turkey with his friend J.-P. It sounds like night after night in the car, arriving in unknown towns at one in the morning, 11,000 kilometers in twenty days, all of which I would find impossible. At first I feel like talking about my work problems, but as always when I anticipate talking about something, I become self-conscious and say nothing. Finally I dispose of the matter (which should have constituted a whole conversation) in a sentence. In comes a group of men, two of whom are bearded fifty-year-olds, twins from the look of them, Nature making a second attempt at what she botched the first time; one of them waves to me—the Argentinian from yesterday (at the Flore); the other, I have some vague recollection, is an art critic. At another table, beyond them, we are amazed to see two boys eating together: they look poor, badly dressed, sickly, one seems to be North African, the other, wearing dark glasses, has the coarse, dirty hands of a laborer. What are they doing here? Two men who work together, splurging?

I am glad that all I have to do is get home and climb into bed. On the radio, a reedy woman's voice without vibrato, boring and "retarded," connects a Beethoven sonata (but it is played by the jailed Argentinian: a touch of demagogy) to an endless recording of some Japanese speaker, then, no less endless, the harsh voice of an Indian singer. All this as if it were perfectly natural: crazy, boring programs, with obscure transitions. I continue with pleasure the *Mémoires d'outre-tombe*, in which I have reached the "Hundred Days."

27 AUGUST 1979
(change to perfect tense)

I wait for Philippe S. at the Select (the Coupole is closed for August); the terrace is crowded, I find the café unpleasant—perhaps because it isn't one of my haunts; a woman by herself—a pickup? No, she leaves without saying a word. Behind me, a nicely pitched woman's voice, speaking to a guy who must be making a pass; something about a horoscope; they are looking for the right signs to match Sagittarius, which must be the guy's sign; comically, they all match, "even Taurus." The waiter is talking with a customer, his attention is not to be attracted until he has carefully finished his sentence, the way one folds one's napkin (Proustian scene: the customers' bell ringing in the kitchen). We go to the Rotonde for dinner, in a booth; next to us, a very excited little old fellow is making (another) pass at a younger woman, missing a few teeth. Philippe and I talk about Chateaubriand, about French literature, then about Éditions du Seuil. With him, I always feel euphoric, full of ideas, confidence, and excitement about work; he encourages my old notion of writing a history of French literature (according to Desire). I make the mistake—a bizarre, uncustomary idea—of ordering a pear brandy with a second cigar and extending the evening; whence a rather intense stomachache. I walked home alone. Everything deserted this August Sunday at eleven at night. Rue Vavin, I passed a young, lovely, elegant, elaborately made-up woman walking her dog; she left a delicate scent of lily of the valley behind her. I skirted the Luxembourg, the Rue Guynemer empty as far as I could see. On a kiosk, a huge poster for a film; the actors' names (Jane Birkin, Catherine Spaak) printed in huge letters—as if they were incontestable attractions (but what do I care about Catherine Spaak, do you think I would cross the street to see Catherine Spaak, etc.). In front of 46 Rue de Vaugirard (a sort of general headquarters of Protestant activities), an attractive boy, who goes in before I can get much of a look at him. In bed, without forcing myself to read the contemporary chores, I get on with Chateaubriand right away: amazing passage about the exhumation of Napoléon on Saint Helena.

Always this difficulty about working in the afternoon. I went out at around six-thirty, for no good reason; in the Rue de Rennes noticed a new hustler, hair in his eyes, a tiny earring; since the Rue Bernard-Palissy was completely deserted, we discussed terms; his name was François; but the hotel was full; I gave him some money, he promised to be at the rendezvous an hour later, and of course never showed. I asked myself if I was really so mistaken (the received wisdom about giving money to a hustler *in advance!*), and concluded that since I really didn't want him all that much (nor even to make love), the result was the same: sex or no sex, at eight o'clock I would find myself back at the same point in my life; and since mere eye contact and an exchange of words eroticizes me, it was that pleasure I paid for. Later in the evening, at the Flore, not far from our table, another hustler, angelic with his long hair falling on either side of a part down the middle of his head; now and again he glances at me; I am attracted by the way his white shirt opens down his chest; he is reading *Le Monde* and drinking a Ricard, I think; he doesn't leave, finally smiles at me; he has coarse hands, which belie the sweetness and delicacy of the rest; it is from his hands that I deduce his hustlerdom (he ends up by leaving before we do; I stop him, because he smiles, and make a vague rendezvous). Down the street, a whole noisy family: three or four children, all hysterical (always, in France): they wore me out, even at a distance. — Back home, on the radio, I heard about the IRA attack on Lord Mountbatten. Everyone is outraged, but no one mentions the death of his grandson, a boy of fifteen.

Urt, 31 AUGUST 1979

Wedged into the wicker armchair, smoking my cigar, watching TV. . . Rachel and M., who had gone out for an after-dinner stroll, have come back to take me with them, the evening is apparently so lovely. At first I was annoyed: what, not a minute without someone asking me for something, even if it was for my own good! Then I went with them, regretting my irritable impulse, especially since M. is so affectionate and so naive, so sensitive to anything lovely, as Mam used to be. The late twilight was of an extraordinary beauty, almost strange in its perfection: a fleecy pale gray, not at all melancholy, banks of mist on the other side of the Adour, the road lined with tranquil houses and flowers, a golden half-moon, crickets chirping, *as in the old days*: nobility, peace. My heart filled with sadness, almost with despair; I thought of Mam, of the cemetery where she was, quite close by, of "Life." I felt that romantic impulse as a certain value, and I was sad at never being able to say so, "always worth more than what I write" (theme of the course); in despair too at not feeling at home either in Paris or here or traveling: no real refuge.

Paris, 2 September 1979

Back from Urt yesterday afternoon; plane crammed with a
stupid public: kids, families, a woman next to me vomiting
in a paper bag, an adolescent bringing back a pelota racket.
Slumped down in the seat, without even loosening my safety
belt or making a single move for over an hour, I read some
of Pascal's *Pensées,* recognizing in "man's miseries" all my
sadness, my heavy heart at U. without Mam (all this really
impossible to write: when I think of Pascal's dryness and
tension). Landing in Paris, everything was heavy, gray. Dinner that evening with J.-L. (Y. not there): he had made a
roast (overcooked), there were avocados with a very black
vinaigrette, French and Spanish melons, bread from Mono
prix in a plastic bag, and wine in a carafe. Darlame talked a
lot (very fast, a little drunk on the wine); I realized after a
while that this was more or less for my benefit (to seduce
me); for a long while there has been some sort of dispute
between us, and now, for the first time, there was a positive
act of speech on his part; but I was embarrassed by the presence of Eric M. and J.-L. P. When I left, early, he wanted to
leave with me; in the elevator, I kissed him, rested my head
on his shoulder; but whether this wasn't his sort of thing,
or because of some other reticence, he responded only
vaguely. I accompanied him in the taxi, he holding my hand,
as far as Clichy (crossing Paris). At table, we had talked
"about women." That evening, exhausted and enervated, in
bed (radio impossible: ultramodern music, sounds like rabbit
turds) I read the personals in *Libération* and the *Nouvel Ob-
servateur*: nothing interesting, nothing for "old hands."

3 SEPTEMBER 1979

The Deux Magots having reopened, there are fewer people
at the Flore; almost empty inside. I read, looking up often,
but still getting something out of Pascal's *Pensées*. Nearby,
an excited group (I've seen them before): fashion queens
and in the middle a tiny hysterical girl (she is showing them
pictures, talking, buttering toast, all her fingers high in the
air). To a newcomer, a pretty boy, peacocking: "You have
such big feet" (I could look at nothing else, in white socks).
Renaud C. passes, all in blue, eyes, shirt, everything; I've
never known anyone less metaphysical, that is, more
"ironic" (with the slightly disagreeable quality this implies);
also François Flahault and Madeleine with her huge eyes;
embraces coming and going; she must think this a bit much.
Jean-Louis P. doesn't want to eat at the Flore (no doubt he
resists being seen there with me, that is, passing for "kept,"
given the difference in our ages). We dined, uncomfortably,
at La Malène. I know that André telephoned him from
Hyères and that what he really wants is to join him there,
leaving tonight, in fact; out of generosity, perversity, fatal-
ism, seigneurial swagger, I convince him to go. He leaves
at nine, and I am alone, quite sad—determined to give up
(but how to tell him? wouldn't it be shameful to stop seeing
him, on the excuse that . . . ? but that is what I'd like, eager
to clear my life of all these messes). I went back to the Flore
to continue my Pascal with a cigar. A tall dark hustler I know
by sight came over to say hello, sat down, ordered a lemon
juice and water; his name is Dany, he's from Marseille; very
low class, has difficulty expressing himself. I feel he is depressed; he's just out of the army, waiting to begin training

for industrial design; he has no place to live and complains constantly; moves from one friend to the other, picks people up in the station or at friends', etc.; if only he had a studio; in short, he's in deep shit. For the rest, typical hustler's language: that is, rather chaste, in which the thing itself is never mentioned. Each time I insist, in order to make him say he's ready to go to bed with me, he answers: "I'm free." I wake up in the middle of the night—five o'clock; I think bitterly and sadly of my relation with J.-L. P.

5 SEPTEMBER 1979

Tired of working, I go out earlier than usual; not wanting to go to the Flore, where I have a date at eight o'clock with F. W. and Severo, I went to the terrace of the Royal-Opéra to read *Le Monde*; the cars are back, the evening no longer has the August emptiness I so enjoyed. Alone, upset, a hustler I know named José, a pale long-limbed boy with light blue eyes; I avoid him, for once again I have forgotten to bring him the signed book he asked me for (I can't imagine who told him that I wrote), and each time he insists; besides, I want to read my paper; I end up by talking to him; now he's working at the Continental; I ask him: "Is it good there?" thinking of the clientele; he answers that when it's no longer dark (thereby telling me that because of his situation he knows a few secrets), it's not very clean, despite the modernistic look of things. With F. W. and Severo, dinner at Bofinger. Leaving the restaurant and walking toward the car parked at the base of the statue of Beaumarchais (Severo keeps saying that he wants to live here), F. W., in one of his occasional fits of solemnity and affection (I am always in dread of them, knowing he is going to talk to me about myself with all the interest of a fond Judge, and I immediately feel myself becoming an evasive child, changing my body), using for transition my comment about that book *M/S*, about which I had said—and what else could I have said—that this universe was absolutely inaccessible to me—F. W. announces that one of these days I'll have to explain myself about the rejected aspects of my sexuality (in this case, sadomasochism), about which I never speak; I feel a certain irritation at this: first of all, quite logically, how could I explain myself about what does not exist? All I can do is *report*; and then, it's so discouraging, this fashion—this doxa—of constituting sadomasochism as a norm, as normal, so that any failure to acknowledge it has to be explained— accounted for. — From the beginning of the evening, Severo was obsessed with checking out a bar he had heard about in the Rue Keller, near the Bastille—a leather bar. Since he never lets go of such notions, we walk there, F. W. and I secretly hoping that we find nothing at all; in the Rue Keller, discovered after we come upon a charming perspective of apartment buildings, a round steeple (Notre-Dame d'Espérance?), an orange window, a real piece of Italy, the bar is garishly lit, nothing clandestine about it, shouts can be heard coming out of the open door, the place is filled with blacks, one of whom is gesticulating and threatening the manager, also black. Relieved, we give up. The night is mild. Back to the car, the neighborhood full of young men. I feel like walking but my stomach is bothering me a little (though I had talked up Bofinger, generalizing the necessity of going to good restaurants so to avoid being sick), and I don't want them to stop the car in front of my house—for with F. W. and Severo I never do, and habit is like a minor superego. Coming home alone, I climb the stairs and pass my own floor without realizing it, as if I were returning to our apartment on the fifth floor, as if it were the old days and Mam were there waiting for me. An exceptional oversight that disturbs me. Read in bed the statements by Khomeini: dumbfounded! It's so "scandalous" that I don't dare be outraged: there must be a rational explanation for this anachronistic madness; it would be too easy just to laugh at it, etc. In short, *Paradox* calls.

7 SEPTEMBER 1979

At the Flore where, exhausted, I argue painfully, parsimoniously—perhaps because neither the text nor the boy, very tense though good-looking, attracts me—with Jean G. about his novel (I offer a few comments to show that I am cooperative, but I have the impression he takes them "personally" and closes up), an old Moroccan hustler (Alami? Alaoui?), whom I knew at least ten years back and who since then, each time he sees me, tells me the story of his life and hits me for money, appears, begins telling me some grim tale about an inheritance (a woman who was in love with him has died, leaving him a villa in Cannes, but there are problems, the police suspect him of being a pimp, etc.), and actually sits down at our table to tell the details in greater comfort. I refuse (his rudeness gives me the energy to refuse); he makes an angry gesture and knocks over chairs in his abrupt departure. That evening we go to the little

Chinese restaurant in the Rue de Tournon with Bernard G. and his (new) Italian friend, Ricardo; at first nothing much, but gradually he appeals to me because of a kind of bodily freshness (hands, chest in the unbuttoned white shirt): the trio of Desire inevitably forms, B. G. having, by his choice, designated *whom I should* desire. I envy their being together and going to Vienna tomorrow. I leave them tenderly—but a little bitterly, as far as I'm concerned, since they're going away for a long time, and besides, in any case . . .

8 SEPTEMBER 1979

Last night, dinner at La Palette with Violette. At the next table, a black man eating alone: sober, silent, discreet; a civil servant? To end his meal he orders a yoghurt and tea. The evening is warm, the street full of people and cars (monstrous procession of motorcycles). I extend it by heading around eleven for the Flore, unprofitable; a rather wretched type sits down beside me and immediately begins talking to me. Annoyed, I bury myself in my paper. Very difficult to read one's paper in peace.

9 SEPTEMBER 1979

Evening: not much to tell: at Restaurant 7 with friends; a good moment, despite the stupid environment: heavily made-up old women, gaudy clientele showing off. But earlier in the afternoon of this Saturday, a kind of insatiable cruising: first of all at the Bain V, nothing: none of the Arabs

I know, no one interesting, a lot of nervous Europeans; the only exception, an Arab, not young but not bad, interested in Europeans. Apparently without asking for money, he touches each one's cock, then moves on to the next; who knows what he wants? Pure paradox: an Arab for whom someone else's cock exists and not only his own (which is his ego). Interminable, prolix monologue (not a conversation at all) of the owner, who describes his disappointments in a Tunisian hotel (wretched food and all the young Tunisians impudently cruising him, he explains, hypocritically disapproving). It occurred to me to go looking for a hustler in Montmartre; which is perhaps why, in bad faith, I found nothing at Voltaire. Very stormy sky, heavy raindrops, a lot of cars. At La Nuit, absolutely nothing (exploding the rumor that it's hot at five in the afternoon). Then appears a tall dark fellow with a rather strange, somewhat delicate countenance; his French is coarse, I take him for a Breton; no, his mother is Hungarian, his father a White Russian (?), in short a Yugoslav (very mild, very simple). Mme Madeleine, whom I had been told was very sick (an infarct), appears, huge and limping out of her kitchen, where an eggplant is lying on the table; she introduces a handsome Moroccan who is quite willing to make contact and gives me a long stare; he will wait in the dining room until I come back down, seems disappointed that I don't take him right away (vague date for tomorrow). I leave light-headed, physically at ease; still following my notion of a diet, I buy a loaf of very crusty bread (a sober but not a self-denying diet) and nibble at the heel; the crust crumbles in the Métro, while I make complicated transfers—but I persist, determined to find out the barometric pressure, Avenue Rapp, in order to regulate my new barometer. In the taxi on the way home, storm and heavy rain. I hang around the house (eating some toast and feta), then, telling myself I must lose the habit of *calculating* my pleasures (or my deflections), I leave the house again and go see the new porno film at Le Dragon: as always—and perhaps even more so than usual—dreadful. I dare not cruise my neighbor, though I probably could (idiotic fear of being rejected). Downstairs into the back room; I always regret this sordid episode afterward, each time suffering the same sense of abandonment.

10 SEPTEMBER 1979

Yesterday, late in the afternoon at the Flore, I was reading the *Pensées*; at the next table, a thin boy with a very pale, glabrous face, good-looking and strange, unsensual (fake leather trousers), busy copying phrases and diagrams from a notebook onto loose sheets; couldn't tell if it was poetry or mathematics. The hustler Dany, black eyebrows and red sweater, came over and sat down beside me, drank a lemon juice and water, he says his stomach is bothering him, eating too much fast-food—and sometimes not eating at all, during the whole day; he still has no place to live; his heavy hands are moist. Outside the sky is stormy, there are drops of rain—and no taxi, of course. With Saul T., not at all eccentric tonight, a grey suit, a red shirt, we decide against Bofinger and go to the little Chinese restaurant in the Rue de Tournon. Saul seems depressed and the evening lags, I'm bored enough to be interested in our neighbors: an opulent black girl at whom the little Vietnamese waiter makes an

abrupt pass, two Frenchmen, one of whom is quite handsome; he has set his wallet and keys down on the table beside
him; the other man goes downstairs to the toilet twice; they
talk about tennis, pronouncing with a strong French accent
the words *Flushing Meadows*, *Wimbledon*, and are drinking
rosé. Yet it was the evening when the proposition made in
July was to be settled, Saul was to give me his answer. But
I no longer desired him, I was tired, without even the energy
to finish the matter. I said nothing about it, as did he, of
course. After all, that's what a double answer is. Excellent
method to erase desire: a long-term contract; it drops of its
own accord. In bed, finished Renucci's *Dante*; awful! I got
nothing out of it.

12 SEPTEMBER 1979

At the American cocktail party for Richard Sennett (admi-
rable: a whole sociology in the fact that he cannot express
himself in another's presence, as if expression were a self-
evident higher value), where I find Edgar Morin, Foucault,
and Touraine, trapped (we were told it was a cocktail party,
it was a debate), I was thinking of nothing but my date with
Olivier G. We went to Bofinger for dinner, but it seemed
not so good this time, and not so pleasant, more expensive,
too many people, the champagne not chilled enough, etc.
Afterward we walked slowly down the Rue Saint-Antoine
and the Rue de Rivoli, it was mild, a little misty, deserted
(these are daytime neighborhoods). I was faintly apprehen-
sive about how we would say goodnight (still hesitating
about the management of Desire), but at the same time feel-

ing relaxed. We had been having a good conversation, and Olivier seemed comfortable (what fine eyes he has!). We took a cup of tea in a café on the Place du Châtelet; it was a bit odd. The separation went easily enough; O. didn't want to come back to the house—which I had anticipated, and I was afraid of that anyway (because of my desire and because I was sleepy); we made a date for Sunday lunch and separated in the Place du Châtelet; he didn't kiss me, but I wasn't hurt by that as would once have been the case. I walked home, taking the Boulevard Saint-Michel and the Rue Saint-André-des-Arts; tired as I was, I still wanted to see boys' faces; but so many were so young that I began to feel depressed. Le Dauphin was empty except, at the end of the terrace, for one black boy, with long, delicate hands, in a red jacket.

14 SEPTEMBER 1979

Futile Evening. Stormy and not at all warm: rainy, hostile wind; I didn't know how to dress for such weather; finally I put on a blue windbreaker, bought in New York, practically brand-new (I have replaced the zip-in lining); it fits badly, the sleeves are too long and there is no inside pocket, so I feel crammed with objects, at risk of losing them—the way I lost my cigar case from this same jacket; already I am not comfortable this Evening. At the Museum of Modern Art (a grim neighborhood), there is an opening of Pleynet's painters; I am surprised to find the pictures absolutely splendid, radiant, full of color; the ones that bore me are the ones I know, the theoreticians, the sad ones (Devade, Cane, De-

zeuze); there are a lot of people, the usual vernissage conversations. ("There's a lot of shit on the walls, but not all,"
remarks one gentleman in glasses, scribbling something in
a notebook: an answer, probably timid and insincere, to two
beefy fellows who prowl through the show with a provoc-
ative hostility.) I see Sollers, Pleynet, then sneak off, never
able to look at an exhibition long. I walk a while toward the
Pont de l'Alma with Lucien Naise: very nice, but I can't man-
age to enjoy his remarks (though flattering, unconditionally
so—or because of that? for this compels me to squeeze up,
and I don't like the feeling that my answers are curbed), or
(especially) his body, a little sweaty, not very sensual. I am
already paralyzed by the boredom of having to attend the
opening of Pinter's *No Man's Land*—perhaps because of my
windbreaker; I hesitate. I'd like some champagne, which I
stop and order at the bar of Chez Francis; this is a restaurant,
and the bar is just for the waiters, who add up their bills and
count out their bank notes. I take the Métro, as though on
my way to a chore. Boulevard Bonne-Nouvelle, everything
is grim; the weather is cold now, humanity depressed, the
neighborhood full of pretentious and sordid little restaurants
(with overdecorated chairs), as well as third-run or porno
movie houses. Since I was fifteen minutes early, dismayed
at the idea of waiting in a first-night audience, with my
jacket, not knowing what to do, figuring that a cup of coffee
wouldn't take me fifteen minutes (in cafés as grim as these),
I walked down the Boulevard; which was fatal to Pinter, for I
decided not to retrace my steps (actually: no *consequence*); I
wanted to go to the Flore, but it was too early and would
have made too long an evening; I looked for a movie: nothing appealed, or else the film had already begun; then I

found one theater where they were showing Pialat's film about kids passing their *baccalauréat* (J.-L. had said it was wonderful, in his way, of course, which means aside from any esthetic criterion, and according to affective-intellectual impressions that concern himself exclusively). The film, though perfect and justifying all the praise it had received, was instantly painful to me: I don't at all enjoy realistic descriptions of social "milieu"; there was a sort of "youth" racism (one felt absolutely excluded), it was abusively hetero, and I don't like that very contemporary sort of message in which you have to sympathize with down-and-outers (limited horizon of the young, etc.), and where the whole universe is idiotic: the arrogance of the derelict, so much for our times. Leaving the theater and heading toward the Opéra, groups of young people; a girl says something just like what I had been hearing in the film. The film is "true," since it continues in the street. Arriving at Saint-Germain, just above Le Drugstore, a very handsome white hustler stops me; I am stunned by his beauty, the delicacy of his hands, but, intimidated and exhausted, I claim I have an appointment. At the Flore, beside me, two Laotians, one too effeminate, the other attractive in his boyish way: some friendly conversation, but what use is it? (Still exhausted, I want to read the paper.) They leave. Painfully I make my way home, dazed by a migraine, and continue Dante, after taking an Optalidon.

17 SEPTEMBER 1979

Yesterday, Sunday, Olivier G. came for lunch; waiting for him, welcoming him, I had manifested the solicitude that usually indicates that I am in love. But as soon as lunch began, his timidity or his remoteness intimidated me; no euphoria of relation—far from it. I asked him to come and sit beside me on the bed during my nap; he came willingly enough, sat on the edge of the bed, looked at an art book; his body was very far away—if I stretched out an arm toward him, he didn't move, uncommunicative: no obligingness; moreover he soon went into the other room. A sort of despair overcame me, I felt like crying. How clearly I saw that I would have to give up boys, because none of them felt any desire for me, and I was either too scrupulous or too clumsy to impose my desire on them; that this is an unavoidable fact, averred by all my efforts at flirting, that I have a melancholy life, that, finally, I'm bored to death by it, and that I must divest my life of this interest, or this hope. (If I consider my friends one by one—except for those who are no longer young—it has been a failure each time: A., R., J.-L. P., Saul T., Michel D. —R. L., too brief, B. M. and B. H., no desire, etc.) Nothing will be left for me but hustlers. (But then what would I do when I go out? I keep noticing young men, immediately wanting to be in love with them. What will the spectacle of my world come to be?) —I played the piano a little for O., after he asked me to, knowing at that very moment that I had given him up; how lovely his eyes were then, and his gentle face, made gentler by his long hair: a delicate but inaccessible and enigmatic creature, sweet-natured yet remote. Then I sent him away, saying I had work to do, knowing it was over, and that more than Olivier was over: the love of *one* boy.

Designer:	Sandy Drooker
Compositor:	Wilsted & Taylor
Text:	11/13.5 Fournier
Display:	Fournier
Printer:	Malloy Lithographing
Binder:	Malloy Lithographing